THINGS EVERY KID SHOULD KNOW

CHEATING

UMAR NURI

1

Cover Design by Madeeha Shaikh

THINGS EVERY KID SHOULD KNOW

CHEATING

UMAR NURI

3

Dedication

'(Our Lord! Accept this from us; You are the All-Hearing, the All-Knowing).'

(The Qur'aan: Chapter 2, Verse 127)

Max and Ali were two friends who lived next door to each other. Ali was ten and Max was nine and they both liked to study.

However, one Friday, the teacher told Max's entire class that they would have a biology test on Monday; something he wasn't happy about because he did not want to spend his entire weekend studying.

After the bell rang at the end of class that day, Max picked the answer sheet from the teacher's desk and slipped it into his backpack.

When Max got home he went to his room to put his book bag away. He took the answer sheet and put it under his pillow; he changed his clothes then went downstairs.

When he got downstairs his mom was cooking macaroni and cheese. He set the table and his father came home from work and they all sat down to eat. As they were eating dinner Max was asked how school was.

"I have a Biology test on Monday. I am sure I will pass," Max said with confidence.

After Max washed the dishes and cleaned the table he went to his room to read a book, and then went back downstairs to watch some T.V. He wasn't worried about the test. He knew that he would get an A.

Ali also ate dinner with his family, and quickly cleaned up and was already studying away in his room. He knew that Saturday and Sunday would be his fun days, so he began his studying on Friday night.

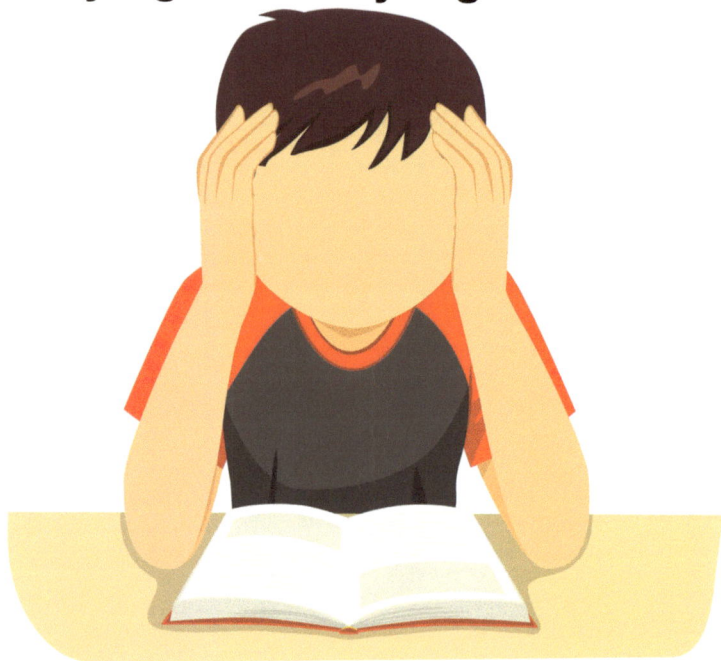

"Ali, do you want some dessert?" his mom asked.

"No, Mom, thank you! I really want to study right now for my Biology test which is on Monday," Ali explained.

Max went to Ali's home on Saturday to see if he could play.

"Hi, Ali, do you want to play?" Max asked.

"No, Max, I must study as the test is on Monday and later today I have some plans with my family," Ali politely declined.

Monday came, and Ali and Max sat at the library before class.

"Max, are you ready for the Biology test today?" Ali asked.

"Yes, I am ready. I think I will get an A on it," Max replied confidently.

"Wow! That's great. You must have studied hard," Ali said.

Max just stayed quiet.

They got to class, and Max went and sat at his table and took the answer sheet from his backpack and put it under his notebook. When his teacher came and gave the test out he took the answer sheet from under the notebook and put it under the test papers; so that he could look for the correct answers.

When the teacher came around Max quickly hid the answer sheet under the test papers. As the teacher walked around she noticed that Max was looking around and looking back and forth through papers. She thought something looked fishy.

The teacher came over to the desk and asked, "Max, what were you looking at?"

"Umm…nothing…my test," Max answered sheepishly.

"What is under your test papers?" the teacher enquired.

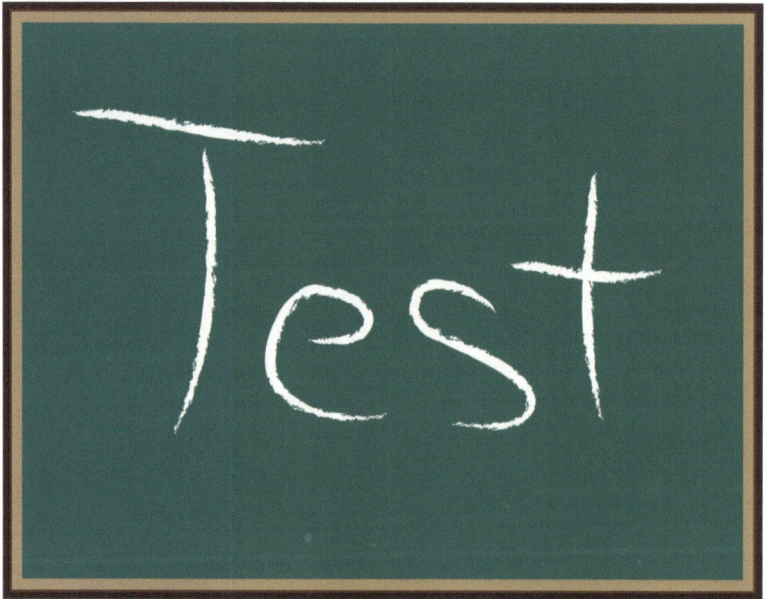

Then the teacher took all of Max's papers from his desk to her desk. She noticed that her copy of the answer sheet, which she had been looking for all weekend, had been stolen by Max and he was using it to cheat on the test.

She called Max to her desk.

"Max, why were you cheating?"

"Because it was hard, and I didn't want to waste my weekend studying," Max replied.

"Max, do you know the penalty for cheating on a test?" asked the teacher.

"Nooooo…" said Max.

"The penalty is I have to give you an F for this test, and the principal will call your parents and tell them what you did. If I catch you doing it again, you will be expelled from this school. Cheating is not permissible and it will not be tolerated at all. Do you understand, Max?" said the teacher.

Max was sent to the principal's office to wait for his mom to come. She had to speak to the principal and then take him home.

"Sorry, I promise I won't do it again, mom. I am really sorry," Max said as he ran upstairs. Soon after his mom went into the kitchen to make dinner, Max went to his room and sat down thinking about how his day passed by and how sorry he was for doing the wrong thing.

Suddenly the doorbell rang and he rushed downstairs to see who it was. When he got downstairs his mom was talking to his best friend, Ali.

"Sorry, Ali, Max cannot play today because he did something bad, and he is grounded," his mom said as she closed the door.

Max asked, "Why can't I play with my best friend, Ali?"

"Because you did something very bad at school today, don't you remember?" his mom reminded him.

Max was very upset and ran to his room and locked the door and he stayed in his room until he heard his dad driving up the driveway. Max ran outside to meet him.

When his dad saw him he said, "Hi, Max, how was school today?"

"It was fine, dad. I missed you, dad!" Max said.

Max and his dad went inside to help get dinner ready. After they sat down at the table, his mom began telling his dad about how he cheated on a test at school today.

"Max, is this true? Why would you cheat, Max?" his dad asked.

Max looked down and said, "Yes, it is true. It was a very hard test, dad."

"I am sure it was hard, but you didn't even study. I would rather you get a B after studying than an A by cheating, Max. In life you don't get far by cheating. I don't ever want you to cheat again. If you need help ask your mom or me, and we will help you," his dad said.

"Okay, dad, I won't ever cheat again," Max said apologetically.

What is cheating?

1. To act dishonestly or unfairly in order to get an advantage in life.

2. Passing an exam or game without putting in effort.

3. To take a test by having the answers at the time of the test.

Why do people cheat?

1. Because they are lazy.

2. Because they want to get good grades.

3. Because they want to boast.

4. Because they don't want their parents to be mad at them.

5. Because they are stressed.

6. Because they don't think it's wrong.

7. Because they are busy.

8. Because it is easy.

9. Because they see everyone else cheating.

10. Because they feel they are entitled to the best.

How to Stop Cheating?

1. The 1st thing that each kid should think about is that Allaah (God) is watching.

2. Fear Allaah (God), that even if you don't get caught in this world, you will have to answer God in the hereafter.

3. Study early on for quizzes and tests.

4. Study with your parents, friends or siblings.

5. Make study sheets and review them daily.

6. Get a tutor if the subject is hard.

Have You Bought The Series: "Things Every Kid Should Know: Drugs, Alcohol, Smoking, Bullying, Junk Food and Amr's Adventure in Europe" for Your Kids By Author, Alya Nuri?

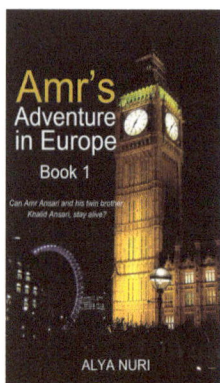

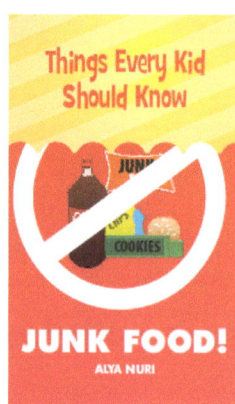

Amr's Adventure in Europe — Book 1
Can Amr Ansari and his twin brother, Khalid Ansari, stay alive?
ALYA NURI

Things Every Kid Should Know
DRUGS!
ALYA NURI

Things Every Kid Should Know
ALCOHOL!
ALYA NURI

Things Every Kid Should Know
SMOKING!
ALYA NURI

Things Every Kid Should Know
BULLYING!
ALYA NURI

Things Every Kid Should Know
JUNK FOOD!
ALYA NURI

Have You Bought The Series: "Things Every Kid Should Know: Strangers, Reduce, Re-use & Recycle, Fire and Muslim Boys" for Your Kids By Author, Abu Bakr Nuri?

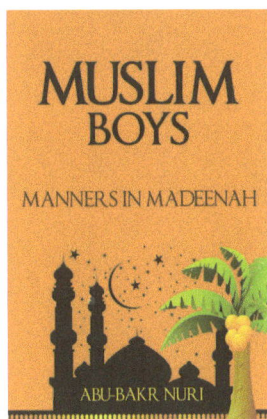

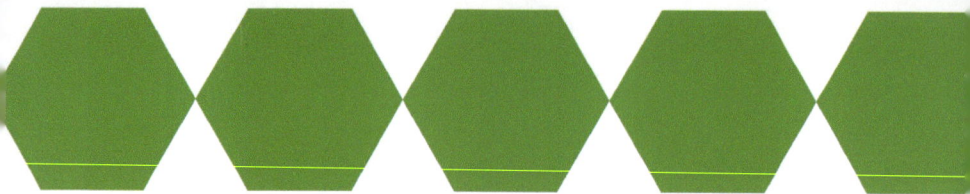

34

www.ingramcontent.com/pod-product-compliance
Lightning Source LLC
Chambersburg PA
CBHW041307020426
42331CB00001B/2